MW01716124

I FEEL, FEEL, FEEL about Moving Away

- A Book to Validate Feelings about Moving Away -

Written & Illustrated by
Jane Un, M.S.

Childswork Childsplay
A Brand of The Guidance Group
CALL 1.800.962.1141
www.guidance-group.com

I FEEL, FEEL, FEEL about Moving Away

A Brand of The Guidance Group
1-800-962-1141
www.guidance-group.com

ISBN: 978-1-58815-151-3

Printed in the United States of America.

How To Apply The Book

Read the book aloud with your child, and ask which feelings he/she can relate to. Ask the child to state an example of what makes him/her feel those specific feelings. Also, ask how often and what specific events provoke the feelings and their coping skills to deal with them. Also ask your child which feelings he/she cannot relate to.

Expand the conversation by addressing the questions in this book or by discussing when he/she has felt the specific feelings outside of the context of the book. Do not judge or challenge their feelings, but validate their feelings. For example, "You must have felt really sad when_______. It must have been hurtful for you to deal with that. I would have felt that way, too." *Let them own their feelings, and for you to accept them.*

Model your own personal feelings about the issue to normalize the feelings or to bring awareness of the differences in individuals in how they may feel. Lastly, discuss suitable coping skills that can be applied when various feelings arise.

Moving away makes me feel
EXCITED & INDIFFERENT

Moving away makes me feel SAD

Moving away makes me feel JITTERY

Moving away makes me feel
SCARED

Moving away makes me feel
ANGRY

Moving away makes me feel CURIOUS

Moving away makes me feel

ADVENTUROUS

Moving away makes me feel

SAD ANGRY EXCITED CURIOUS SCARED INDIFFERENT ADVENTUROUS JITTERY

I have many different feelings about moving. These are all my feelings, and **I am allowed to feel, feel, feel!** This is a big change for me, and it is okay to have all these different feelings.

Expressing my feelings allows me to unload the feelings inside of me. Too many intense feelings inside can make me explode. Acting out on my feelings by breaking rules or hurting others is not okay. I can use my positive coping skills and talk to a trusting adult about how I feel so I don't let my feelings explode. This is a big move for me, and it is okay to have all these different feelings.

I can talk to:

Objective of I Feel, Feel, Feel about Moving Away

I Feel, Feel, Feel about Moving Away helps to identify various feelings, promote validation of the feelings, and provide positive coping skills to deal with the feelings. Effectively transitioning to a new environment may take time, patience, and family effort.

This book can help you learn more about your children, foster closer relations by understanding how they feel, and promote better communication between you and your children. This book is an initial stepping stone for a child to identify feelings, learn positive coping skills, and feel validated about moving away.

Questions

1. Name someone who you trust and feel safe to talk to.
2. What feelings did you relate the most with from the book? And what feelings did you relate the least with from the book?
3. Identify any other feelings that you may feel that are not described in this book, if able.
4. The character on the cover of the book was wearing sunglasses because he didn't want to show others how he felt. Why do you think he wanted to hide his feelings? Why is it unhealthy to keep our feelings hidden?
5. Does your body feel different when you have so many feelings inside of you (ex: feeling hot, tense muscles, fast heartbeat may be clues of anger to some people)? If so, what are some clues that your body is saying, "Hey! I need to unload these feelings inside of me, and use a coping skill to express them before I explode."?
6. With the help from an adult, write down or think of your own positive coping skills for each of the feelings from the book.
7. What makes your new home unique and special?
8. Identify three positive qualities for your new home.
9. Identify three positive qualities for your new neighborhood.
10. Identify three positive qualities for your new school.
11. Describe three things that you look forward to.

Notes to Adults

Moving away can be a difficult transition for school-aged children. Regardless of the reason for the move being positive (e.g. better job employment of the parent) or not, it is still hard because children don't like change. School-aged children endure stressors of a new school environment, making new friends, and adjusting to a new community and social group when they move away. They may have mixed feelings about moving away, as feelings of excitement about the unknown may arise or contrasting feelings about all of the changes.

It is important for your children to be able to communicate how they feel, and for the parent to listen and acknowledge their feelings. These are their feelings, whether it is one feeling or several feelings all at once. We need to let children know that it is acceptable to have various feelings without challenging them or placing judgment. AVOID JUDGEMENT AND CHALLENGING THE FEELING. In other words, you want to avoid "Don't feel mad," as most parents can make the mistake of telling this to their children when something upsetting has occurred. The truth is, what they are feeling is real. It is similar to someone telling you, "Don't be angry" when you didn't get the promotion that you have been working towards for the last five years, to telling your child, "Don't feel sad, it's okay," when he/she didn't get invited to a birthday party that he/she desperately wanted to go to. The point is that the statement is not going to make the feeling disappear or help the situation. In contrast, it's invalidating how one feels. The goal is to validate the feelings so one has been heard and acknowledged.

Continued on the following page >

Notes to Adults (continued)

Parents often complain that their child is not behaving appropriately. Children's behaviors are a result of communicating how they feel (e.g. an angry child will communicate through tantrums). Remember, it is the feeling that is acceptable, not the maladaptive behaviors. You want to redirect the maladaptive behaviors by providing coping skills to use when various feelings arise. Therefore, the child can learn to identify, communicate appropriately, and apply positive coping skills to deal with their feelings, as well as feel validated.

If possible, it is suggested to discuss with your child the changes to expect, and to engage in similar social activities as in the previous environment. Talk to your child about the positive changes that will occur, and any concerns he/she may have about the move. Role model an "adventurous" presence to your child, as it may help to elicit optimism in your child. Be careful not to invalidate their feelings, and provide opportunity to explore benefits.

It is important to mention that each child will react differently to transitions. Some children may have more difficulty in dealing with transitions than others. It is important to seek professional assistance if your child is experiencing behavioral and emotional problems that are disruptive.